**Boost Your Child's Confidence In School and in Life**
By Jean Young

EXPERIENCE
EVERYTHING
P U B L I S H I N G

## Disclaimer

This document is geared towards providing exact and reliable information in regards to the topic and issue covered. The publication is sold with the idea that the publisher is not required to render accounting, officially permitted, or otherwise, qualified services. If advice is necessary, legal or professional, a practiced individual in the profession should be ordered.

- From a Declaration of Principles which was accepted and approved equally by a Committee of the American Bar Association and a Committee of Publishers and Associations:

The information provided herein is stated to be truthful and consistent, in that any liability, in terms of inattention or otherwise, by any usage or abuse of any policies, processes, or directions contained within is the solitary and utter responsibility of the recipient reader. Under no circumstances will any legal responsibility or blame be held against the publisher for any reparation, damages, or monetary loss due to the information herein, either directly or indirectly.

The information herein is offered for informational purposes solely, and is universal as so. The presentation of the information is without contract or any type of guarantee assurance.

The trademarks that are used are without any consent, and the publication of the trademark is without permission or backing by the trademark owner. All trademarks and brands within this book are for clarifying purposes only and are the owned by the owners themselves, not affiliated with this document.

Introduction

Section 1: Ways To Boost Your Child's Confidence

Section 2: Ways To Help Your Child Excel In School

Section 3: Ways To Boost Child's Confidence For Better School Performance

Conclusion

## Introduction

A child that has a good level of self-confidence is able to face the world and all its challenges with a more optimistic approach compared to that of a child that lacks self-confidence. Children who are aware of their weaknesses and strengths while still feeling good about themselves find it easier to deal with negative pressures and conflicts.

On the other hand, a child who does not have much self-confidence is likely to say they cannot do it the moment they encounter any new challenges. They do not think highly of themselves and they often question their worth. Feeling that they are not good enough is a normal occurrence for these children. They find it difficult to look for solutions to their problems. When left alone with this feeling of being inadequate, they will either get depressed or be withdrawn.

There are many things that can affect the development of a child's self-confidence. The most important factor that influences a child's confidence is their parents, especially during the early years of their life. Parents who accept their child for who they are, are giving their children a good foundation to begin with when developing their self-confidence. However, children will start thinking of themselves as incapable or not having enough skills if one or both parents criticize too much.

Being too protective of your children is not good for them either. You need to let them learn to do things on their own so that they can learn to be independent which is important for the development of their self-esteem. If adults still make mistakes, so do children. They are still in a phase where they are still learning about their environment and everything else that goes with it. A parent who is able to accept and love their child exactly as they is also teaches the child to accept himself. And it is a good way to get the child started on developing their self-confidence.

Sometimes, children lack self-confidence not because they do not have the right abilities. Instead, it is because of the ridiculously high standards that their parents or the society has set for them. Even their friends can have a huge impact on the development of their self-confidence. Sometimes the power of friends to influence a child's self-confidence is even greater than that of the parent's.

Confidence can mean different things to different people. But when we talk about a child's confidence, it includes:

- believing in that they can do things
- truly believes their self-worth
- being responsible for their actions
- having an optimistic outlook of life

Now, one confident child will be brave enough to speak in front of the class, act on stage and talk to teachers. While another confident child may prefer to stay quiet in their seat and keep a few close friends. Though they appear to be different, they are both confident in the sense that they are both willing to learn new things.

Let us further discuss the components of self-confidence as mentioned above.

*Believing That They Can Do Things*
A child that believes in what they can do despite not being really great at it has a better advantage over a child who has better skills but lacks the confidence to do things. When you truly believe in your skills to do something, you are more likely to motivate yourself to do it. Therefore, you are able to make your beliefs come to life. This is helpful not just in school but in all aspects of a person's life.

*Truly Believes Their Self-worth*
Self-worth is not about what others expect you to be or how they see you. Neither is it about what you have achieved. Rather, self-worth refers to how a person values their true self. When you truly value yourself, you know the kind of value that you have for others and you know and accept who you truly are. A child that truly believes in their self-worth knows that they are unique and they understand the unique role that they have in this world. They truly know who they are and they accept themselves for who they are.

When a child knows their self-worth, they will not give up just because they failed and neither is it going to discourage them from trying again.

*Being Responsible For their Actions*
We do not just mean taking the blame if something goes wrong. When you are responsible for your actions, you know that any success or accomplishment that you have is because of you and your abilities. You do not blame it on luck or destiny. You know that whenever a situation arises, you have a choice. Instead of being reactive, you are proactive.

*Having An Optimistic Outlook In Life*
If you want to be confident then you need to have an optimistic outlook when it comes to your life, the people around you and your environment. A person with an optimistic outlook sees a half-full glass instead of a half-empty one. They know how to look at the brighter side of things even when the situation does not seem so good. So when you encounter a difficult situation, you learn to brush it off as something that is not too important. You learn to look for the positive side of a situation. Instead of will study being depressed about failing an exam, you will be able to tell yourself that you will pass next time because you are going to study harder.

On the opposite side, a person that has a pessimistic outlook on life sees a glass as half-empty. This person tends to think that things will not go too well for him. It is easy for them to get anxious about situations that are challenging and they is more likely to get depressed as well.

How does confidence affect your children's performance in school?
A child may have problems with their performance in school. Sometimes the struggle that they goes through has nothing to do with the skills they have but rather it is a result of their lack of confidence. Children that are confident are not afraid to ask teachers any questions or clarifications. They tend to participate more often in class activities and discussions and it is easier for them to mingle with their classmates and teachers.

On the other hand, a child that lacks confidence is making themself fall even further behind by not asking any question or participating in the class activities.

Is there anything that you can do to help improve your child's confidence so that they can boost their level of confidence? Yes, there are things that parents can do to help their children boost their self-confidence so that they can perform better in school. You will learn more about the things that you can do for your child in the next sections.

## Section 1: Ways To Boost Your Child's Confidence

As a parent, you are going to be a powerful influence on your child's self-confidence. How you treat your child and how you respond to them has a great influence on how confident they are going to be. It is common for parents to protect their children as much as they can but you also need to make sure that you are not overprotecting them. You also need to give them some space so that they will learn to fend for themselves and slowly wean themselves from being too dependent on you or your partner.

There are many ways that you can help your child gain more confidence. By following the tips that you are going to read below, you should be able to boost your child's confidence in no time. When your child is confident, they will be able to perform better in school and in life as well. Your confident child will find it easier to deal with challenges compared to a child who lacks self-confidence. Instead of saying no or *'I cannot do it'* to every challenge that comes their way, they will find ways to overcome their challenges without being depressed or anxious about it.

What are the different ways that you can do to help boost your child's confidence?

1. When your child learns something new, give them the chance to practice their new skill so that they will be able to master that skill. You will need to be really patient with them though. Children do not learn as quickly as adults do. And when we say chance to practice, it means lots and lots of opportunities and not just a few tries before you expect them to be a master of a new skill.

Sometimes a skill that the child wants to learn seems to be complicated. Or something you would consider that children at this particular age should not be learning just yet. If your child wants to learn how to bake cookies by the age of five, then let them although you will probably need to supervise them to make sure they don't blow up the house. When you do supervise, make sure you are doing just that and not doing the baking yourself. Let your child do the dirty work.

The good thing about this is if a child faces a challenge, they will not get discouraged. They will be able to recall the other times they managed to overcome other challenges and that will give them the confidence. They know that even though something is difficult, they will still be able to overcome this new challenge.

2. Children are children and they will always make mistakes. Do not beat them up for it, literally or figuratively. Instead of giving them a sermon about what they have done wrong this time, gently talk to them about what went wrong, why it is wrong and the ways that they can improve to avoid making the same mistakes. Don't tell them that they are stupid or good-for-nothing. Instead, give them words of encouragement and tell them to just try again. This is a good way of training them how to deal with any challenges that they encounter in life. You are teaching them to be confident enough to try again after making mistake and to keep going.

3.   Your child is so excited that they have learned to ride the bike without the training wheels and they just cannot wait to show you. Or maybe they just learned how to write their full name in school. Yes, now that you're all grown up, these things are a piece of cake. It's not something you'd be thrilled about. But this is your child we are talking about that is learning a new skill. It's all new for them and it's exciting. You can encourage them to keep learning new skills by being enthusiastic every time they wants to show you what they has learned for the day. Even if you have had a bad day, muster up the excitement even if it is just for your child's sake. But usually, it is easy to get excited about something a child does for the first time so it should not be that hard.

4.   Each child is unique. Each child has their own set of unique talents and abilities. Don't be comparing your child to your friend's child. And in order for your child to gain more confidence, help them identify the things that they are good at, the skills that they have. A child might feel bad for not being able to do something. To make them feel better about himself and to help them gain some confidence, point out something that they are good at.

5.   It is important that even at an early age, you instill a very important message to them which will help them especially when life starts getting more complicated. Convey to your child that they will be able to achieve the things that they want to achieve if they are persistent enough. They might not get it the first time around but trying again is worth it because they might be able to succeed the second time around. And if they still can't then a third attempt might be all they need. Persistence is the key.

6.   Take some time off from your busy day every day to spend some quality time with them. This is a good way for them to know that you love them and you appreciate them. A child who feels loved and appreciated feels better about themself and it is a good way to boost their confidence. The time that you spend with them is not counted by how long you spend time with them. But what's more important is the attention that you give them. It is better to spend an hour with your child with your gadgets away from you so that you can pay attention to them alone than being with your child for hours while you constantly check your email or text messages.

7.   As a parent, it is important for you to be a positive role model for your child. You are a person that the child looks up to and whatever you do, the child is likely to imitate. So if you have low self-confidence yourself, it is time to boost it up. You cannot possibly expect yourself to be a good teacher on self-confidence if you cannot walk the talk.

8.   It is easy to give praises to a child when the end result is a successful one. But what if they failed? Regardless of the results, it is important for parents to praise the effort a child is exerting in order to achieve something. By doing so, you are letting a child know that no matter what the results are, you still love them and that you appreciate the effort that they are showing.

9.   There will be times that certain activities can only be done at certain times. You need to make this clear with your child and to have a set of rules that both of you should stick to. Say for example playing basketball. If you have a playroom for your child, you need to let your child understand that playing basketball is only allowed in the playroom where they won't be breaking things like your favorite vase. Or if you don't, a child needs to understand that bouncing and throwing balls should only be done outdoors. They need to understand that not everything they want to do can be done whenever they want to because there are certain rules that we all need to abide by.

Another example is if a child wants to cross a street. At a much younger age, like 3 or 4, a child needs to understand that they have to be accompanied by an adult to cross the street. But when they is a little older, you need to teach them the rules before crossing the street: Stop, Look and Listen. They need to understand why such rules apply. In this way, you are allowing them to be comfortable about the things that they should be doing which is going to be a good confidence booster!

**Section 2: Ways To Help Your Child Excel In School**

Just like their confidence level, you can also help your child excel academically with your support and guide. What are the different things that you can do to help your child perform better in school?

1. It is important that you attend parent-teacher conferences. Parent-teacher meetings are the best way to know more about your child's performance in school and to talk to their teacher about the different things that both you and the teacher should be doing to help your child do better in school. There are things that you may not know about your child that the teacher can inform you about and there are things that you know that a teacher might find of good use to be able to deal better with your child. This is also a good way for your child to know that anything that happens in school can also be shared at home. If your child has any additional or special learning needs, meeting with their teacher more often might also be useful for your child.

2. Isn't it just so confusing when your child talks animatedly about how their school day went but you find it hard to relate to the things they are telling you because you do not know where the things are located or who they are talking about? If the school has a website, make sure that you take the time to check it out. You should be able to find the names and pictures of the school staff. You might even find a layout of the school so that you know where places like their classroom, the playground and cafeteria are located. Or if you cannot find that information online, you can simply take a tour of the school and get to know the people your child interacts with regularly.

Other important details that you should be able to find on the school's website are:
- Contact information for the staff
- Calendar for the school year
- Any upcoming events at school
- Testing Dates

Teachers might also have their own websites where they post things like assignments, projects, any class activities and trips.

3.   Homework is a good way to reinforce the things that a child has learned in school. So it is important that you provide any support that your child needs as they do their homework. There may be instances when a child does not clearly understand the instructions or cannot seem to have the right answer. Be there to guide them or her but do not answer the homework yourself.

It is also important that you enforce a study/homework period every school night. This is a good way to reinforce good study habits in your child and it will help them do well in school as well. You should also provide the child an area that is conducive for learning. The room a child is doing their homework in should be well-lit and free of anything that could distract them.

4.   Your child should be all set to learn when you send them off to school. This means that your child should have breakfast before going to school. You definitely don't want them missing out on class because of a trip to the nurse due to stomach pain caused by hunger. They will also be more energetic when they have eaten breakfast. The breakfast that you give your child should also be nutritious and low in sugar.

And for a child to stay focused and not be sleeping during school hours, they need to get the right amount of sleep. A child that gets a good night's sleep is less irritable and is more likely to have a better disposition in the morning. So make sure that your child gets at least 10 hours of sleep in a day.

5.    Organizational skills are necessary even for a young child. This skill is not something we are born with. But rather it is something that we learn along the way. When you are organized, you will spend less time looking for things and spend more time on more important matters. With your child, you can help them get organized by getting a homework folder for them so that it is easy for you and them to track the assignments that they have for the day. You could also teach them how to use a calendar when they can write already and help them create a list of things to do. They don't need to be as complicated as the ones we adults create. The organizational skills that you are teaching them will not just be helpful in school but also when they grow up.

6.    Children are going to have exams every now and then and teaching them the right study skills is also important. Even at a young age, they needs to understand that they will be able to do better in exams when they studies several days before the exam instead of cramming the night before. As a parent, it is important that you help your child break down the different topics that they need to study for an exam so that they won't get overwhelmed by it. You can also help your child learn the right study materials that they need to bring home for an exam.

7.    You have to familiarize yourself with the different disciplinary policies that the school has. You will be able to find this information in the student handbook. When you are familiar with these rules, share this information to your child so that they are aware of what is expected of them in terms of behavior, attendance in school and so on.

8.    Be involved in your child's school activities. A child needs to know that their parent is interested in them and you can show this interest by being involved in the various activities that the school has organized. If they have any upcoming school trips, you can volunteer to be one of the chaperons. Or you could even read a story to their class when the opportunity presents itself. If they have an upcoming class party, you can help out by organizing the party and preparing for it. If your child has any upcoming concerts, recitals or games then show up in the different activities that they have in school. Being involved with their school activities is a great way to show your support for them.

9.   School attendance needs to be taken seriously. The only reason your child should be staying at home is if they are sick. Otherwise, they need to be in school. However, there will be times when a child fakes being sick to avoid certain things in school. These could also result into real symptoms. If you notice anything unusual about your child's behavior when it comes to school, talk to them about any problems that they might be having with their classmates, teacher and so on. If they have missing too many days of school, talk to the teacher to see what they need to catch up on. And if the child has any anxiety about going to school, talking to the teacher should help you get a better insight on what has been going on in the classroom and what can be done about it.

10. Always take the time to talk to your child about how the school day went. When you have this chat with them, make sure that they have your undivided attention and make eye contact with them. The way you talk and listen to your child is what your child is going to imitate. If you ask them how their day at school went and the things that they did, you are letting your child know that you are interested in these things. It will also make them want to do better in school. The questions that you ask them should not be limited to yes or no answers. Getting younger children to talk about how school went is easier because children at this age tend to be more talkative.

**Section 3: Ways To Boost Child's Confidence For Better School Performance**

The ability of your child is not the only thing that determines how well they will do in school. Did you know that even their confidence level can have a great impact on how well they will do in school? When your child lacks confidence, they are less likely to participate in important school or class activities. They won't have the courage to speak up when the teacher asks them a question even if they know the answer. Or if they do not understand a particular topic in class, they won't even bother to ask the teacher to clarify it because they fear that the teacher or their classmates might make fun of them. This is going to become a cycle that leaves them falling further behind.

So what are the different things that you can do to help them boost their confidence when it comes to school performance?

1. If your child has a skill gap, then you need to help fill in this gap. This is usually a reason why children start to lose their confidence in school. This is especially needed for topics that are prerequisites to further learning. If there is any topic that your child does not quite understand, take some time to help them understand this topic. The first step that you need to do to be able to help them fill this gap is to determine which area or topic they are having problems with. The child's teacher should be able to assist in this. Once identified, it will be easier for you and your child to work out ways to help them catch up.

2.  Giving your child a positive reinforcement is also a good way to help your child regain their confidence. There are parents who have set high standards for their children that bringing home an exam with one or two mistakes is not enough to get them acknowledgments or praises. Make sure that you do not make the same mistake because this is one sure way to kill whatever confidence your child has left. Even if they does not get a perfect score but has managed to make good improvements from their last exam and has a passing score, make sure that you provide praise for this. Getting positive reinforcement from you, their teacher and even their classmates is a good way for your child to boost their confidence.

3.  It is important to have homework and study time if a child is to excel in school. When a child spends time every day, even if it is just an hour, reviewing the day's lesson and studying their homework, they are already doing a lot to boost their academic performance. Yes, life is hectic and we have a million other things that we need to do in day. Even a child has a list of things that they want to do in a day. But no matter how busy you and your child are, make sure that you spend some time to sit down and study or do any homework for the day.

Another good way to do study time is to coordinate with the other parents in the class and set up a group study. This will encourage your child to gain confidence in discussing projects and assignments with other people and it is also a good way to exchange ideas and to learn to help each other out.

4.  If your child has things that they need to learn to fill in their gap which you cannot quite handle, you can always hire a tutor for your child. The great thing about tutors is that their teaching style or method can be customized so that it will meet your child's learning abilities. A tutor will also give your child the undivided attention that they needs since a tutor will only need to focus on your child, their strengths and weaknesses which is unlike that of a teacher who has to focus on all her students. Tutors are also capable of providing positive reinforcement for your child whenever applicable. Your child might not also be ashamed to ask any questions if there are any things or subjects that they do not clearly understand because it is just them and the tutor.

## Conclusion

When a child has better confidence in themself along with great skills, they will surely excel in class. They will no longer be ashamed to speak out in front of the class. If there are any school activities, they won't hesitate to sign up for them and they will also understand that it is okay to ask questions when needed. They know that asking questions whenever they need to make clarifications is not going to make them a lesser student. Rather, they understand that it is a way to enhance what they already know or to help them understand what they do not understand.

There are various ways to help a child boost their confidence. The very first things that parents must do in order to build the foundation of their child's confidence is to provide their undivided attention when a child learns something new. And if a child makes a mistake, instead of yelling at them, parents should encourage children to try again. It is okay to be protective of your child but you need to allow them to do things for themself in order to learn. Children will make mistakes and they need to understand that it is okay to make mistakes. What is more important is that they try again. That is the only way that they will be able to gain more confidence in themself and to be independent.

Setting aside some study/homework time and learning great study habits will also help your child perform better academically. As a parent, it is your role to teach them these study habits. These skills that they learn in elementary school can also be applicable when they reach high school and even beyond that. You are teaching them a good value. In order to achieve things or to succeed, you need to put in some effort and persevere. Success does not happen overnight but rather it is something that you work hard for. This is something that they will be able to apply not just in school but when they work and even in their goals for themselves. So not only are you boosting their confidence so that they can do well in school but you are also teaching them lifelong skills.

EXPERIENCE
EVERYTHING
P U B L I S H I N G

www.ingramcontent.com/pod-product-compliance
Lightning Source LLC
Chambersburg PA
CBHW071811020426
42331CB00008B/2460